PILLOW

NO MORE SEX: ONLY LOVEMAKING

TALK

PILLOW

NO MORE SEX: ONLY LOVEMAKING

TALK

A Kingdom Prescription to
Physical and Spiritual Union

Biblical Keys to
Intimacy, Unity, and Ecstasy

DR. DAVID B. MILLS

Cover and interior layout and design by David "3D" Ferreira of MASTERGRAFIX.com.

Editing by Sonya D. Ferreira of Thoughts & Prayers at ThoughtsnPrayers.com.

First Edition - 2012

TABLE OF CONTENTS

FOREWORD

When it comes to the area of physical intimacy many Christians have made the transition from the kingdom of darkness to the Kingdom of Light pertaining to their spirit but many have not transitioned relationally, financially or physically in their intimacy. And just like in the natural realm pillows are where we rest, relax, recline and release for oneness. Just as when there are things in the midst of the pillows we rest on, they end up becoming things of separation and disunion, even division. So there are things inside and in between us hindering incredible oneness and closeness. Some of our pillows include irons which are things that have not been ironed out. Maybe there are Xbox controllers where we still are playing games emotionally and physically in order to control family members. Maybe there is money in our pillows and financially when times are hard or money is tight they cause us to hold back physically. Maybe our pillows have phones in them. Our intimacy is interrupted by all the connections we have in the midst of our oneness such as girlfriends as well as male friends that we allow to cause division. Maybe our pillows are in homes that have gauze and bandages over the hurts, scars and wounds which are in the way of two becoming one flesh! Maybe we need to have a Pillow Talk?

One of the best biblical illustrations of the heart behind pillow talk is found in Luke 9:58 when Jesus says the Son of Man has no place to lay his head. In this text, Jesus says "foxes have holes, the birds of the air have nests but the Son of Man has nowhere to lay His head." He wasn't just talking about a place to rest his head physically, but he was referring to a place to download his heart, mind and spirit to produce and reproduce intimacy, family and destiny. When a husband and wife come together they are sharing their hearts, spirits, minds and yes their bodies in a process of oneness. There is union, revelation and expression given through these actions.

Another pillow process that reveals oneness is in Genesis 28. Jacob is on the run but he stops and makes a rock his pillow. There heaven is open to him and in the midst of a rest stop there is an opening for Pillow Talk. What is a pillow when there is a process where there can be Pillow Talk? Pillow Talk is communication, instruction and wisdom released for new levels of oneness, agreement and assignment. It is a process as we learn to talk and communicate in any area we can grow in that area. Understand sex is your gender not how you are to please one another! First Corinthians 7 says, "Husbands care for things of the world and how he may please his wife." First Corinthians 7:34 says "Wives care for things of the world and how she pleases her husband. Lovemaking is supposed to be a pleasure fest! Let's start some Pillow Talk!!!!!!!!!

INTRODUCTION

There are some sacred issues among today's Christians that keep us from experiencing what Jesus called us to have...an Abundant Life! In John 10:10 Jesus is not just talking about having abundant life in a religious vacuum. But I believe Jesus wants us to have abundant life in every area realizing all of our life in Christ is spiritual and relational. Therefore all of it whether it is worship, parenting, vocational, financial and even the physical are to be abundant in totality. Four major problem areas of thoughts and mindsets about lovemaking are:

(1) Worldly mindsets and precepts: While many have been delivered through salvation, most people have not transformed their mindsets when it comes to relationships. They have not discarded, disentangled and divorced themselves from customs, old motivations, intentions learned from family, community and society that may not have been God's mentality.

(2) Wrong concepts and thought processes: The truth is if we still are doing things the way we did without Christ or without a biblical reference, the best we can get is what the rest of the world gets and not a Kingdom experience!

(3) Ignorance: Our own ignorance is only limited to what we are not willing to learn. In the same way one's level of production is limited to one's instruction, it is true that one's level of satisfaction is limited to one's level of instruction and communication (Hallelujah...it can CHANGE!)

(4) Lack of Biblical instruction and education: There are some things that cannot be totally and openly shared in a church congregation setting, it's just not wisdom. So how do we deal with areas of our life that are generally not discussed openly? God is so awesome in that the same way He connects and communicates with His church for her instruction, direction and satisfaction is the same thing He does for us. He uses people to write His plan and purpose for us that we might be able read, apply it and be empowered to fulfill His plan and have good success.

The word of God says in Hebrews 13:4 "Marriage is honorable and the bed undefiled, but fornicators and adulters will be judged." First of all, this scripture informs us that lovemaking is to be reserved only for those who have made a holy covenant and any other practice would come with the results of some form of judgment. Now the judgments may not be with thunder and lightning bolts and can manifest in different forms. It can be disease to one's body, an unwanted pregnancy or the financial weight that affects the next relationship including soul ties internally. It may be undesired lasting memories that battle one's future relationship and unity. These reasons explain why God wants us to walk in

DR. DAVID B. MILLS

abstinence prior to marriage so none of us would have to deal with these results. But if you are dealing with these results, the God of heaven even has an answer for all of those affected by past issues, it's called confession and forgiveness.

Two of the greatest things you can do if you have suffered through these issues is ask God's forgiveness and forgive yourself. Forgiveness is the best gift you can give yourself and your mate so you can access a greater level of oneness. This book is written by a man that learned all the wrong reasons, mindsets and concepts that were geared to a man's own satisfaction of himself. It was and still is a totally self-centered, selfish practice of the flesh and a malchovinistic mindset. Only because of Christ's love with biblical teaching, leading and searching do I understand that lovemaking is intended to be pleasing (fulfilling the wishes and desires of our mate). Only then are we fulfilling God's intentions in marriage. Brothers and

INTRODUCTION

Sisters, it's time we make the shift from No More Sex: Only Lovemaking!

PILLOW **TALK**

NO MORE SEX: ONLY LOVEMAKING

CHAPTER 1

IT'S NOT SEX...
IT'S LOVEMAKING!

Someone said a long time ago to be careful what you call a thing because that's what it will become. Over and over the Bible tells us in Romans 12:2 be not conformed to this world but be transformed by the renewing of your minds that you may prove what is that good and acceptable and perfect will of God. The truth is many times Christians, and people in general, believe it only applies to religious processes, church or routines. People believe it applies to salvation of our spirits but not the order and honor of our relationships. The word of God will only work to change our lives in the area it is known, understood and applied. If I do not know what the word says about singleness in 1 Corinthians 7, I am left with whatever mindset or concept I had prior to Christ. This includes possible views of singleness as time lacking and rejection rather than interpreting singleness as the gift of being unique, whole and complete. So it is with lovemaking without a biblical view. I am left with a street, hood or worldly perception and family history of "booty calls, tapping that, getting some, getting laid, hitting it or having SEX."

First, sex is a description of one's gender not God's intention of how to please or satisfy one another. How a person defines a thing is usually how they display and demonstrate a thing. Second, God never calls lovemaking sex. The word sex is never mentioned in the King James Version of the Bible. He never used the word sex because he never intended to describe it that way. Remember sex has to do with one's physical nature and gender not the God-given goal of pleasing each other. All of those other names and descriptions are all about physical activity not geared or focused on creating new levels of unity, intimacy and ecstasy!

It also must be noted that there are many different terms used biblically that carry a separate mentality, weight and different end. Here are some examples of terms used in a biblical context in place of sexual relations:

Took - seize, use, fetch, get. It connotes physical activity but not an intent of action or satisfaction of both persons. (Genesis 34:2)

Went in - to go or come, employ to get, to pull in, intercourse en route. It is not focused on dual release. (Genesis 16:4)

Forced - to depress, afflict, to deal with harshly, defile, humble, rape, date rape. (1 Samuel 13:12)

Lay with - ravish, sexual connection, cast down. (Genesis 19:35, 1 Samuel 12:4)

Benevolence - conjugal duty, kindness, well-minded, reconcile. (1 Corinthians 7:3)

DR. DAVID B. MILLS

Knew - observation, recognition, with care, answer, consider, discern, discover, come to give, skillful. (Genesis 4:1)

As you see this one activity can have a multitude of different mentalities and a plethora of motivations and intentions. It is to this end that this book is written. My heart is to have every family in God's Kingdom operating in its highest, greatest and best level relationally instead of operating in religion, quiet frustration, isolation, division or distraction. Just know it's NOT sex because sex is one's gender not how God intends for us to fulfill one another!

CHAPTER 1
QUESTIONS:

IT'S NOT SEX, IT'S LOVEMAKING

1. Where did you get your perception or views of physical intimacy?

2. What is sex?

3. What is important about how we define a thing?

4. According to 1 Corinthians 7:32, what is the goal of the husband?

5. According to 1 Corinthians 7:34, what is the goal of the wife?

6. Husbands ask your wife, how can I please you? (Please take notes)

7. Wives ask your husband, how can I please you? (Please take notes)

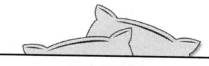

CHAPTER 2

HOUSTON, WE HAVE A PROBLEM

When it comes to getting to a place of unity, intimacy and ecstasy there can be many hindrances. Medical sciences have found how to create physical stimulants like Viagra, Cieara and the rest. While man has come up with physical medicines there are some issues not even medicine of the greatest doctors can handle. Only God the Father is capable of handling some issues. We have to understand the concept of our entire person being in alignment to produce maximum enjoyment and not (as many a man thinks) that being intimate is in another component.

Here is an illustration to help explain the total connection. Our body is to tied to our spirit and our spirit is tied to our soul. Similar to a bike, if the pedal is the spirit the soul is the chain and the body is the gear box. They all are necessary for us to get to our intended destination called the "O" zone. It is imperative that we understand that each part affects the other parts. We view the chain as links of what we do verbally, linked to what we do emotionally, linked to what we do mentally, linked to what we do financially, linked to what we do as a family, linked to what we do physically.

Any chink in any one of the parts will affect and can hinder our ability to reach intimacy, unity and ecstasy. Some of these areas that hinder us are:

Issues of Past Hurts - These hurts are and can be big or small. There are situations and conditions that are open and need to be addressed to have forgiveness and closure. You both can go through the motions and still have sex but not lovemaking without

Sell your books at sellbackyourBook.com!

Go to sellbackyourBook.com and get an instant price quote. We even pay the shipping - see what your old books are worth today!

Inspected By: socorro_gomez

00071940451

addressing these hurts. While there may be physical moments there is not the highest level of freedom or enjoyment from oneness when past hurts linger.

Issues of Frustration - Frustration has a lot to do with one's focus, tension, emotions, and issues pertaining to fear, insecurity and inferiority. This why it is necessary to have a open spirit and clean soul because they affect the body. Issues of the heart, mind, or just distractions and sometimes physical problems that are tied to different seasons in one's life. Communication will be key in resolving these problems and if you need to see a doctor, they have wisdom in this area also.

Issues of Unforgiveness - As long as there is unforgiveness in a person's heart, there will be a spiritual block on their heart and what God will release from heaven. Understand even lovemaking is a spiritual act that involves the anointing and the anointing always honors what is in order. Forgiveness means to cause a release therefore unforgiveness can be a road block to a release.

Issues of Bitterness - Bitterness can cause a lack of ability to produce or release. In 1 Samuel and Micah it describes bitterness as pain, hurt and unforgiveness that we allow to reside, abide, grow and fester in us. No wonder it hinders us from experiencing oneness.

Issues of Burdens - There are times when the cares of this world can hinder a word to us and a release from us. When we allow situations and conditions to rule in and reign in our mind, heart or spirit they become hindrances to oneness. Our body may be present but our mind and heart could be absent. The weights of kids, money, or bills can only rob us if we allow them to steal the thrill of being in unity, intimacy and reaching ecstasy.

Issues of Fatigue - I'm just tired! It's okay to be tired sometimes but two, three or more times in a row can start trouble and serve as notice that there is something more to your fatigue. There are times we must help our mate by helping them rest. Allow them to go take a nap. Let them retire early, run a bath, and their rub feet. If these don't help, it may be time to exercise and maybe even see a physician. Check your calendar and schedule time to stop!

Issues of Lack of Trust - This issue is usually only because there have been other issues (be honest). If there is hesitation there is usually a reason. Communication and truthfulness are best when there have been issues of infidelity because there will be areas of a lack of trust. We are reaping from what we are sowing either way. Now patience, faith and love has to grow and be healed again. Even when we sin and ask for forgiveness, Christ forgives us but we have to deal with and accept the consequences from it. Patience, patience, patience. You have to give each other time to heal.

Issues of Unfaithfulness - It has the same affects as the lack of trust. While there may be forgiveness the hurt, pain, resentment and rejection are real. It is unfathomable to ask someone not to have emotions, express the impact, or embarrassment of unfaithfulness. It penetrates, and cuts relationally, mentally, emotionally, physically and in the psyche of a person. Counseling is mandatory not an option!

Issues of Sin or Being Sinned Against - Regardless of the circumstances of the sin the answer must begin with repentance and a willingness to bring forth fruit (mat). According to Matthew 3:8 we should have evidence (bear fruit) of repentance. Confession is agreement to sin but repentance looks and focuses on doing different (repantancevs). If there is no knowledge of a different mindset or process, behaviors will be repeated.

Issues of Fear - Fear of inferiority, insecurity, lack of knowledge and fear of performance. A lot of times fear is a negative, inward assumption of a problem. Sometimes fear is internalized to the point one is paralyzed by one's own unproven expectation. In 1 Timothy 1:7 it states faith takes steps to try without known results. Are you in fear or in faith? They cannot exist at the same time.

Issues of Dishonor - When we or our mate belittle, disregard, devalue, minimize the others' communication, opinions, emotions or conditions we dishonor. When these behaviors happen publically, especially in front of or around other people, it will create a void for intimacy.

Issues of Neglect - Frankly leaving our mate to their self to meet their need for communication, affection, attention and not showing, expressing, or investing in them for a period time results in neglect. What is not cultivated will not grow and will not bring forth fruit.

Issues of Disrespect – Behaviors of denying, devaluing, giving degrading responses or lack of response, and making decisions, plans, choices, that do not include, consider, show price of the union, or other person in the relationship.

Issues of Insecurity - Pertains one person's inability to have security and confidence in a mate or their self. There may be issues of mistrust that create insecurity or just a undervaluing of oneself.

Issues of Ignorance - Of all the things that can hinder intimacy and ecstasy, ignorance can be changed just with communication and instruction.

My heart is to tell you even though there are many reasons for hindrances and problems some of these can be handled. You can still reach your mission of pleasing the other person. Ask for forgiveness, talk, strive to be naked and not ashamed like Adam and Eve in Genesis 2. Houston we have lift off!

CHAPTER 2
QUESTIONS:

HOUSTON, WE HAVE A PROBLEM

1. Do you have any hindrances to lovemaking?

2. Is there any unforgiveness, bitterness or other issues blocking oneness with your mate?

3. How are the body, soul, and spirit connected?

4. What is communication?

5. What are two issues that could become hindrances?

6. Are you willing to become naked and not ashamed?

CHAPTER 3

GETTING A KINGDOM PERSPECTIVE
(GETTING OUT OF THIS WORLD!)

When it comes to intimacy, unity and ecstasy many still struggle to renew their minds. They are still driven by selfish desires rather than see lovemaking as a part of our God given ministry. Our prior information and motivation may not match with God's kingdom intention. First Corinthians 7 says His intention of a married man is to please (satisfy, fulfill the desire and wish of his wife). That is a far different mentality than the "gotta get mine, just get yours" mindset from society. Remember salvation and the

Kingdom causes us to renew our minds and have kingdom intentions. So being intimate with our mate is no longer sex, a booty call, getting laid, knocking boots or anything else the world calls it. If we only do what the world does, we will not get what we should in a kingdom experience of unity, intimacy and ecstasy. Do you want the results of the world or the results that come from operating, living and loving from a kingdom position? When God says in Genesis 4:1 "he knew her" he meant man experienced intimacy with her heart, her spirit, her thoughts and her flesh. He knew all of her being not just one part!

Men, sometimes the mindset of our sisters can be a challenge. For so long, they have been told not to have sex because it's dirty which creates a thought pattern causing women not to want sex. Sometimes these thought patterns affect Christian women today causing them to withhold releasing oneself to the fullest and have complete capacity of enjoyment. Hebrews 13:4 gives us God's perspective. The word from the King of the Kingdom is to begin covenant, have fun, experience freedom and His blessing.

The perspective in the Kingdom is to never intentionally leave your mate in frustration, isolation or rejection because the goal is your mate's satisfaction. Men hear me, we are to love our mate and this includes lovemaking in the mindset Jesus had toward his wife, the Church. According to Ephesians 5:25 Christ loved the Church so much he sacrificed himself and disciplined His flesh for her. This means men we have to develop self control and patience then develop more patience according to Proverbs 25:28. When men take the responsibility to make sure we minister (yes it is ministry) to our wives we serve like Matthew 20:28 says, "whosoever is chief let him be servant." This means asking your wife how can you serve her. No greater love has any man than to lay down his life for his

DR. DAVID B. MILLS

friend. We can learn to "lay down our life" by making our satisfaction secondary when it comes to intimacy.

Our wives are made in such a way that even after she is pleased she can still minister to us. God is the greatest designer, engineer, and creator. After a brother satisfies a sister, then he can be satisfied by a sister. (I call this the dying for her satisfaction and the promise of resurrection.) Our perspective must become what they are for the Kingdom. First Corinthians 7:32, 34 shares how lovemaking ought to be an all out pleasure fest with each mate having the goal of pleasing the other. It is opposite of the worldly mindset and process. Remember in Romans 12:2 our prayer should be Lord renew our minds.

We must realize that to the spiritual, all things are spiritual. This means you should pray "Lord help me to please my mate and teach me how to please my mate." Does not the word say ask and it shall be given, seek and ye shall find, knock and it shall be open to you. I want everything to have an anointing, God's favor, order, honor and power. How about you my brother and sister?

Remember our first ministry is our family so take care of your house. The perception that one's body is their own is not in accordance with the word of God which tell us when we agree to covenant, we agree to partner in our assignment. First Corinthians 7:3 states the word benevolent means to give to the needy, satisfy the promise of payment, or satisfy what is required. It simply means that which is to be expected because of commitment, promise, and covenant agreement. I am not saying a woman or man can never say no, but biblically the only reason physical intimacy should be denied is due to prayer and fasting. I understand there are times when fatigue and tiredness are real but this should not occur regularly or by routine. Nobody has a headache a whole week! Neither is it to be used as a tool of manipulation or punishment. Even men in prison get conjugal rights.

DR. DAVID B. MILLS

PILLOW **TALK**

In marriage, no one partner has total authority over their body. When we withhold from one another it's like we put the other person in foreclosure by taking the property of our body until they make a payment of our requirement. Hook a brother up, hook a sister up! The Bible goes on to say "do not defraud" which means to break a promise and not fulfill it. That's like giving your mate a bad check by knowingly depriving and sending them into recession then depression.

The word of God and our obedience to Him becomes our bailout. We get the benefits of the stimulus package and according to the word of God, it is Satan who comes and brings his best distractions. Let me be clear NO MATTER what our mate does or does not do it never clears or frees us to choose to sin. Every choice is a choice of loving Jesus, God's Son, or loving and submitting to sin. And when it comes to sexual sins, 1 Corinthians 6:18 says every sin a man does is without his body; but he that commits fornication sins against his body. So that literally sex outside of marriage is a fivefold sin. According to 1 Corinthians 6, sex outside of marriage is sin against God. Second, it is sin against Christ (6:16). Third, it is sin against the Holy Spirit (6:19). Fourth, it is sin to the person it is done with. Fifth, it is sin against one's own body or self. Besides all of that, sexual sin comes with a promise of judgment from God stated in Hebrews 13:4. Men and women of God's Kingdom let's receive the Kingdom's perspective and disregard the views from Hollywood and Tinsel Town. We must take note that one other real Kingdom perspective is marriage does not exist in heaven because we will be as angels according to Mark 12:25. The marriage relationship we share will only be active while we are on earth.

PILLOW **TALK**

CHAPTER 3
QUESTIONS

GETTING A KINGDOM PERSPECTIVE

1. What does it mean to please your mate?

2. What does it mean when scripture states Adam knew his wife?

3. What is your mindset about lovemaking?

4. Define the Kingdom according to Hebrews 13:4.

5. According to Ephesians 5:25-29, how does Jesus love the Church (His wife)?

6. Lovemaking should be a _____ and _____?

CHAPTER 4

THE RIGHT PURPOSE AND INTENT

Someone said a long time ago "where the purpose of a thing is not known, abuse is inevitable." When it come to the area of lovemaking, many times people have been told it's about getting yours, getting some, or getting mine. All those views are actually selfish, self-centered mindsets only meant to satisfy self. The reality is that when it comes to lovemaking we may need a renewed mind. (Romans 12:2)

The reality may be we have experienced salvation of our spirit, we may not have experienced a transformation in our relationships. An analogy I use is the difference between cable and Direct TV. Both are systems but the difference is that cable is a system that runs underground through the earth in order to fulfill its picture (vision). In contrast, Direct TV is run by another system that is sent down from satellites in space (heavens). A cable system demands the receiver in the earth receive and display its picture. One system is an earthly governed, directed and insulated in natural the realm. A satellite is governed, directed and sent from a heavenly location. So if you want natural results subscribe to cable, but if you want what is out of this world you get connected to another system in Kingdom.

Each system has a contract, receiver and a box. The contract for the kingdom picture and vision is the Bible, the word of God is our covenant. The receiver is the believer, and the box is the Holy Spirit inside that connects, directs and allows us to change. With that, we can have the same equipment and different pictures and futures. The following are

THE RIGHT PURPOSE AND INTENT

Biblical purposes of lovemaking:

1. Procreation (Malachi 2)

2. Kingdom presentation (Ephesians 5 and Genesis 2:22)

3. Physical oneness

4. Physical satisfaction of our mate

5. Removing physical and spiritual distractions to known intimate experience (mind/soul/body).

Biblically speaking if we are to make love the above list should be our goals of reproduction, presentation, physical union, our mates' satisfaction, and removing distractions. Procreation is the means in which God intends to populate the earth. According to Malachi 2:15 there will be a Godly seed in the earth. God intended lovemaking for godly people to multiply His godly seed. According to Ephesians 5:24-25, Kingdom presentation is twofold. It is the portrait over the Church aligning herself for

DR. DAVID B. MILLS

29

His purpose and the portrait of Him giving Himself for life. Together these portraits create a glorious union. According to Genesis 2:22 two becoming one in flesh denotes and connotes the place needed for two individuals to process into oneness of action, emotions, expression, and attention. In I Corinthians 7:33, 34 it deals with satisfaction of the married man and the married woman. God's intention is that husbands please their wives and that as women that you please your husband. Here's the good part, the word please actually means to satisfy, fulfill the wish and the desire of the other (Holla!!!!) **Please note this must be in agreement and comfort for both mates**. God's intent is that when it comes to lovemaking that it becomes a pleasure fest--who is gonna out please the other? (It's getting hot in here!) When considering how to remove distractions the Apostle Paul says it is through satisfaction that we minister to one another to the point we have no wants. Literally, we shut the door on outside lust. Finally, Genesis 4:1 references the "known experience" when

Adam knew Eve physically, emotionally, spiritually, mentally and relationally.

So every time there is lovemaking, we go to new depths emotionally, spiritually, mentally and relationally. According to Proverbs 5:15-21 we are refreshed and blessed which is the Kingdom's purpose and intent. God intends lovemaking to be procreation, kingdom presentation, physical union, dual satisfaction, and a means to get to new levels of intimacy, unity and ecstasy.

PILLOW **TALK**

CHAPTER 4
QUESTIONS

THE RIGHT PURPOSE AND INTENT

1. What happens when the purpose of a thing is not known?

2. What is the difference between cable and satellite systems?

3. To please one another requires _____ and _____?

4. Name some reasons for marriage?

CHAPTER 5

THE PROCESS AND THE "O" ZONE
(TAKING IT TO THE MAX)

Once the intent and purpose is known, then the motivation, application and the goal of satisfaction goes into effect. When we say process, it's intentional. We are not using words like moment, event, or action. A process is a premeditated, planned, patient set of principles or steps in order to reach an intended place. PROCESS- yes this is meant specifically for the brothers (and a few sisters)! Someone once said men are like microwaves and women are like ovens. God's intent is that both be more like crockpots in a process of simmering cooking, boiling, blending and almost exploding. (Selah)

While many men seem to rush out of a lack of patience, ignorance, indifference or wrong selfish expectancy. Lovemaking begins in the morning or maybe the day before not when you get to the bedroom (read that sentence again). We must learn to take our time, slow down, and do ministry (serve) to make our mate our priority. It is ministry to serve those over you, beside you and subordinate to you. According to Mathew 20:28 a chief must be a servant. Serve a brother, serve a sister (tell them you are suppose to serve me BABY!!) Take the time to cause him or her to be mentally, physically as well as emotionally ready. Massage, caress, talk, stroke, hug, cuddle or come up with ways to slowly enter physical intimacy. Implement Proverbs 25:28 and show some self control, care, and apply Christ-like principles. Practice Ephesians 5:25 and give yourself up for her deliverance, then remember Christ's experience after His crucifixion there is resurrection! (Holla)

Our wives are made in a way that once you satisfy her, she can then satisfy you!

There is an eight step process to explosion: communication, expectation, affection, preparation, connection, intension then explosion and restoration. They are called foreplay: 1-verbal foreplay 2-physical foreplay 3-patience 4-entrance 5-process 6-climax 7-restoration. You may ask, how can a pastor teach these things? According to Jesus in Luke 4:18, it is a part of New Testament ministry to deliver people relationally who may be brokenhearted.

One's heart can be set on satisfaction and their own heart is stuck in frustration because what is expected was not given. But the Word says my people perish for a lack of knowledge. Note it is not a lack of anointing or worship but knowledge that people perish. Many times ignorance is what is

DR. DAVID B. MILLS

causing the hindrance. Hope deferred can make a heart sick.

Back to the process, verbal foreplay should start the day before if not that morning. Intimacy begins with a woman's heart and mind long before connecting to her body. Just as God created the world He wanted to enter you should use your words to begin creating the world you want to enter. Depending how old you are it's time to get you rap, find your Don Juan and get your Mack back. For those who may not understand what I just said, it's time to revisit your place of romance. You can share in the evening or morning of the day before. Make a mid-morning phone call or have a lunch time rendezvous. Get creative, leave a card in her car or put it on the mirror before you leave for work (if you have children ask them to put it in her car). Remember confession proceeds manifestation, you got to say a thing before you see a thing. And yes, ladies believe it or not he loves to hear from you too. Let him know what you want. Women are voice activated and men are sight and voice activated!

In Song of Solomon 4:1-5 and 5:10-16 it speaks of physical foreplay. After step one is in place and it is safe and convenient for both of you, the second stage is set. Both partners are to play a role in raising the temperature in each other through massaging, caressing, kissing, stroking, and hugging without entering. The intent should be to cause your spouse to almost overheat, bringing them to a temperature until they can't handle it anymore. Then slowly and methodically, with sensitivity, proceed. The best way to know when to proceed is to watch them for signals (breathing, panting, thrusting or sounds producing sweating) You can ask them, believe me they will tell you. If one is not ready, do your ministry until they ready. Remember it's supposed to be a pleasure fest!!!!

Song of Solomon 4:6, 4:10-11, and 7:1-7 speaks of patience not entrance. Take your time, don't rush, and give your mate time.

Cause your mate to signal you while you learn to control and pace yourself. Before entrance ensure you both are ready then proceed with caution and remember the crockpot and microwave analogy. Let's say you must begin at a pedestrian pace then walk and finally run. It is not a sprint but more the pace of a marathon. It is essential to learn which positions help aid both persons for progression. One position may bring progression, but another may bring explosion. Talk about it and take mental notes. These notes will become your GPS for lovemaking success with your spouse. While in process, pay attention to what are they doing, and take note if what you are doing is working? Notice their eyes/eyelids, breathing, moving, and positioning.

The Process: practice, practice, practice! When you know what to do, keep doing it. (Reference Song of Solomon 2:17, 3:4, 5:2-4, 5:5-6, 6:1-2, 7:8-9, and 8:2-3,14)

During climax first one should notice an increase in breathing, moving, gyrating then continue until one or both clinches or tightens muscles, intensely gripping the other. Notice if your spouse's mouth is opening, eyes rolling in the back of the head, finger or foot cracking, leg and back locking, stiffening, intense thrusting until a feelings of momentary suspension, temporary loss of consciousness, euphoric moments, followed by a internal release and warm sensations. In a woman it can be three to ten contractions during climax.

Climax is similar in a man with the same physical clinching, tightening, increased gyrating until thrusting to point of internal releasing, eyes rolling, mouth opening, sound making, leg locking, back stiffening, foot or finger cracking momentary suspension, and loss of consciousness. This is called an orgasm or climax. (Song of Solomon 4:15-16 and 5:4)

Restoration is the most precious part after satisfying one another. If one is not satisfied, try to satisfy the other, rest and return to step one foreplay. Note: for most men it will

DR. DAVID B. MILLS

take 24 hours to recharge after a release, for some it may take less time. Restoration or afterglow are the moments following climaxing. It is then that women and men are to treasure each other, talk, and celebrate their lovemaking together. They should validate, appreciate and communicate the joy of their experience. (Song of Solomon 1:13)

CHAPTER 5
QUESTIONS:

THE PROCESS AND THE "O" ZONE
(TAKING IT TO THE MAX)

1. What does process mean?

2. When does lovemaking begin?

3. What are ways to slow down the lovemaking process?

4. Name the 8 steps leading to an explosion?

5. Hope deferred makes a _____ sick?

6. Women are _____ activated and men are _____ and _____ activated?

CHAPTER 6

I CAN'T GET ANY SATISFACTION
(PROBLEMS AND SOLUTIONS)

The following lists identify hindrances in lovemaking for men and women. While there are medical stimulants, there are times when they are not even needed and issues of health or the heart are the real culprits. Here are a few of them:

In Men:

1. Alcohol: it is actually a depressant and causes 50% of men to be impotent--

    Solution: Don't drink

2. Fatigue: both emotional and physical causes a decrease in strength and excitement

    Solution: Rest

3. Obesity: usually affects those weighing 250 pounds or more. Weight affects testosterone in men.

    Solution: Exercise

4. Nicotine: a chemical that lowers testosterone

    Solution: Stop smoking

5. Depression and mental affects: one may need to see a doctor, check responsibilities and fulfill them

6. Pressure: chaos, fear or fear of failure can affect a man's performance

   Solution: Focus on pleasing mate

7. Lack of Patience: One may need to stall and delay during foreplay

   Solution: Practice patience

8. Dishonor, Disrespect, and Criticism

   Solution: Encourage, celebrate, and honor one another

9. Anger and resentment

   Solution: Forgive and release

DR. DAVID B. MILLS

PILLOW TALK

In Women (include all those listed above)

1. Frustration: Deal with unforgiveness, bitterness, lack of affection, and preparation.

   Solution: share reason for frustration and talk it out.

2. Self doubt and Criticism: Remember your purpose is to please your mate.

   Solution: Ask how may I please you?

3. Past Thoughts: See unhealthy, past thoughts as sin.

   Solution: repent and release self

4. Weight issues

   Solution: Exercise

NO MORE SEX: ONLY LOVEMAKING

5. Wrong focus: Think of what they need?

   Solution: Focus on others not self

6. Old Mindsets

   Solution: Read Song of Solomon

7. Insecurity: towards oneself or her mate.

   Solution: It takes time to develop trust but you can always try.

8. Neglect: Can be in the form of communication, romance, and non-sexual touch

   Solution: Share what's lacking in the relationship and what you need.

DR. DAVID B. MILLS

PILLOW **TALK**

NO MORE SEX: ONLY LOVEMAKING

CHAPTER 7

POSITIONS EVERYONE!

While intimacy is the main thing, creativity surely keeps the relationship interesting. Please understand it's about both mates so be considerate of each others like and dislikes. But also desire to fulfill, please one another. Here are some but not all positions that bring satisfaction:

1. Submission with female on back, legs open, and male on top

2. Male on back with female with legs spread over him rodeo style

3. Female on her side with right leg lifted and male with right leg through both her legs

4. Rear entry with female on stomach with knee or knees brought forward and arched back and male behind female in-between her legs or with a leg between hers

5. Male in-between female legs- one leg over one of her legs (whichever side bring her joy)

6. Female on her back with legs or heels on male shoulders as male aims and guides himself

7. Take a shower with both individuals standing and male lifting female legs or whole body (you can take it from there)

8. Ask your mate which position causes them to climax, why waste your time? Practice any other position you want, YOU'RE MARRIED!!!! Be creative, don't limit it to a specific room. (Hebrews 13:4)

Everything is better with practice, practice, practice!

DR. DAVID B. MILLS

PILLOW **TALK**

CHAPTER 8

SET IT UP...
PREPARATION THE KEY
TO CELEBRATION

Preparation is the key to every great event, process or purpose and so it is with lovemaking and oneness. The time one takes to invest in lovemaking is valued, appreciated and adds to the excitement that leads to the goal of climax. The following lists are things both can do for preparation towards celebration.

Women: Get ready to be intimate by running a bubble bath, playing soft music, lighting candles, and preparing fruit or apple cider with a massage.

PILLOW TALK

Get into action and consider:

- Lingerie

- Some cute panties

- Spray the bed and the room

- Go bare naked (shock therapy)

- Call him at work (tell him what you going to do to him)

- Get a babysitter

- Make his favorite dinner, feed him then tell him you are dessert

- Find a close hotel close to his job and tell him to come meet you in the room for lunch

Men: Get romantic with rose peddles, candy, soft music, and bubble baths.

Get into action and consider:

- Cleaning yourself up

- Shave

- Lotion your hands and your feet

- Use cologne

- Try a massage, baby oil, poem, and flowers first

- Get a babysitter

- Take her to dinner and tell her you are dessert

- Book a hotel room and tell her to meet you there after work

- Take her on an overnight getaway

- Take her to a local park with a view and her favorite dish, then feed her

- Plan a horse drawn buggy for date night

- Take her dancing

- Check airport to plan a plane ride (tell her you want to give her the sky)

- Take her to the beach for a walk (bring a blanket, sweet, apple cider and glasses)

DR. DAVID B. MILLS

PILLOW TALK

- Send flowers to the job (no reason!!!!)

- Show up at her job and take her to lunch

(Yes men, I gave you more things to do because you are the lead...and need them!)

ABOUT THE AUTHOR

Dr. David B. Mills, is the founder and Senior Pastor of Through The Word Bible Fellowship in New Castle, DE. He is married to his childhood sweetheart Bernadette and they recently celebrated 20 years of marriage, they have five fantastic children. Dr. Mills attended Christian Research and Development under the auspices of Dr. Willie Richardson, where he became a Certified Biblical Counselor. There he also completed coursework for "Pastoring With A Purpose." He has also completed coursework at The Center for Urban Theological Studies (CUTS) through Geneva College. Dr. Mills has received a Doctorate Degree from Minnesota Graduate School of Theology. Finally, he completed Kingdom University under the auspices of Dr. Cindy N. Trimm.

Dr. Mills produced his first book "The Ministry Called Family" where the focus is on restoring families to God's original blueprint. Dr. Mills and his wife, Bernadette have ministered in the Bahamas, Jamaica, Nigeria, Africa and have supported ministry in London, England. They have also traveled the United States ministering on Roles In Marriage, Leadership, Motivational Workshops for Men and Women as well as Youth. Dr. Mills and his wife, Bernadette are the producers of the "TAILOR MADE" Marriage Event that is held at various locations along the East Coast as well as the annual "IGNITE" Valentine Weekend held in King of Prussia, Pennsylvania. They have both been guests on The Trinity Broadcasting Network (TBN).

You can connect with Dr. David B. Mills via:

Facebook: **David B. Mills**
Twitter: **PastorDaveMills**
LinkedIn: **Dr. David B. Mills**
Email: **Throughtheword@aol.com**
Web: **throughtheworddbm.org**

PILLOW **TALK**